T0086852

John Rutter

Lament for the holy city

Flute and piano

MUSIC DEPARTMENT

OXFORD
UNIVERSITY PRESS

OXFORD
UNIVERSITY PRESS

Great Clarendon Street, Oxford, OX2 6DP,
United Kingdom

Oxford University Press is a department of the University of Oxford.
It furthers the University's objective of excellence in research, scholarship,
and education by publishing worldwide. Oxford is a registered trade mark of
Oxford University Press in the UK and in certain other countries

© Collegium Music Publications 2016 and 2017

Exclusively licensed worldwide to Oxford University Press

John Rutter has asserted his right under the Copyright, Designs
and Patents Act, 1988, to be identified as the Composer of this Work

Database right Oxford University Press (maker)

First published 2017

Impression: 6

All rights reserved. No part of this publication may be reproduced,
stored in a retrieval system, or transmitted, in any form or by any means,
without the prior permission in writing of Oxford University Press

Permission to perform this work in public (except in the course of divine worship)
should normally be obtained from the Performing Right Society Ltd (PRS) at
www.prsformusic.com or a local performing right licensing organization, unless the owner or
the occupier of the premises being used already holds a licence from such an organization.
Likewise, permission to make and exploit a recording must be obtained in advance from the
Mechanical-Copyright Protection Society Ltd (MCPS) at www.prsformusic.com or a
local mechanical copyright licensing organization

Enquiries concerning reproduction outside the scope of the above
should be directed to the Music Rights Department, Oxford University Press,
at music.permissions.uk@oup.com or at the address above

ISBN 978-0-19-352374-6

Printed in Great Britain on acid-free paper by
Halstan & Co. Ltd, Amersham, Bucks.

Lament for the holy city
from *Visions*

This version of *Lament for the holy city*, for flute and piano, is an arrangement of an extract from John Rutter's *Visions*, which is scored for upper voices, solo violin, strings (or organ), and harp.

Available on sale or rental from Oxford University Press:

Visions vocal score (ISBN 978-0-19-351318-1)
Visions solo violin part (ISBN 978-0-19-351319-8)
Visions harp part (ISBN 978-0-19-351320-4)
Visions organ part (ISBN 978-0-19-351321-1)

Conductor's scores and string parts are available on rental only from the Oxford University Press Hire Library or appointed agent.

Visions has been recorded by Kerson Leong, the Temple Church Choristers, and Aurora Orchestra, conducted by John Rutter. The recording is on the Collegium label (COLCD 139).

Lament for the holy city is also available in its original scoring for violin and piano (ISBN 978-0-19-352308-1).

Lament for the holy city

JOHN RUTTER

© Collegium Music Publications 2016 and 2017. Exclusively licensed worldwide to Oxford University Press.

Printed in Great Britain

OXFORD UNIVERSITY PRESS MUSIC DEPARTMENT, GREAT CLARENDON STREET, OXFORD OX2 6DP

The Moral Rights of the Composer have been asserted. Photocopying this copyright material is ILLEGAL.

John Rutter

Lament for the holy city

Flute part

MUSIC DEPARTMENT

OXFORD
UNIVERSITY PRESS

FLUTE

Lament for the holy city

JOHN RUTTER

© Collegium Music Publications 2016 and 2017. Exclusively licensed worldwide to Oxford University Press. Printed in Great Britain

OXFORD UNIVERSITY PRESS MUSIC DEPARTMENT, GREAT CLARENDON STREET, OXFORD OX2 6DP
The Moral Rights of the Composer have been asserted. Photocopying this copyright material is ILLEGAL.

48
52
C
mf
f appass.
mf
58
mp
(mp)
63
poco rit.
a tempo
p
D Più mosso ♩ = c.116
liberamente, quasi improvisando
70
mf
rall. poco a poco
74
mp
(molto rall.)
Lento
♩ = 60
rall.
p
pp

18
A
p
mp
mf
mp cantabile
Ped.
24
cresc.
30
f dolce
mp
mf
dim.
mp
35
B
mf
molto espress.
mf

40
pochiss. rit.
f
dim.
f
dim.
Ped.
45
a tempo
mp
mp accompagnando
mp cantabile
50
C
mf
f appass.
f
55
mf
mp
mf
mp
Ped.

60
(mp)
p
mp espress.
dim.
Ped.
65
poco rit.
a tempo
p
p
pp
p espress.
D Più mosso ♩ = c.116
liberamente, quasi improvisando
70
mf
mp
rall. poco a poco
74
mp
(molto rall.)
Lento ♩ = 60
rall.
p
pp
p
pp
una corda